T0160905

Beyond the Edge of Suffering

Other Books by Peter Conners

Poetry
Of Whiskey and Winter
The Crows Were Laughing in their Trees
While in the World

Nonfiction
Growing Up Dead: The Hallucinated Confessions of a Teenage Deadhead
JAMerica: The History of the Jam Band and Festival Scene
*White Hand Society: The Psychedelic Partnership
of Timothy Leary & Allen Ginsberg*

*Cornell '77: The Music, the Myth, and the Magnificence
of the Grateful Dead's Concert at Barton Hall*

Fiction
Merch Table Blues: A Novel
Emily Ate the Wind

Anthology (Editor)
PP/FF: An Anthology

BEYOND THE EDGE OF SUFFERING

Peter Conners

WHITE PINE PRESS / BUFFALO, NEW YORK

White Pine Press
P.O. Box 236
Buffalo, NY 14201
www.whitepine.org

Copyright © 2022 by Peter Conners

All rights reserved. This work, or portions thereof, may not be reproduced in any form without the written permission of the publisher.

Publication of this book was supported by a grant from the National Endowment for the Arts, which believes that a great nation deserves great art; by public funds from the New York State Council on the Arts, with the support of Governor Kathy Hochul and the New York State Legislature, a State Agency; and with funds from The Amazon Literary Partnership.

Printed and bound in the United States of America.

Cover design: Steve Smock

ISBN 978-1-945680-51-9

Library of Congress Control Number: 2021941545

Table of Contents

Section I: *The Last Day of America*

Section II: *A Story About It*

Section III: Beware Deluxe

Section IV: *The Nature of Precarious*

Section V: Epilogue

—*for Aimée*

I.
The Last Day of America

One of you went on a plane today. One of you did not. One of you slept in your bed last night. I was miles away but I know the sour scent of your sleeping breath, the slow roll of your thin eyelids over pale blue. I am your father. I do not know your dreams. The present tense is all that exists between us. I try to live with that. I say you are my son, you are my son, you are my daughter, we three joined in blood, but our dreams must be our own. High on a shelf, beyond where you can imagine, there is a storybook called Trust Comes Hard to a Man Who Was Once a Dreaming Child Left Alone. You may take it down one day. You may leaf through it seeking a happy ending for your loves before they take their rest, as I did mine. Or you may possess the wisdom to leave the book on the shelf. You may know more. My children, I pray you know more.

I pray you no more. Haven't we had enough? It seems like hours contain minutes, but our whole lives remain inside. Our eyes smile while our masks contain frowns. There is no pity in a virus. I want to quote Shakespeare, but I have only the Lizard King: "You cannot petition the lord with prayer." In the wee hours, the minutes of our misspent youth come calling. I want to tell my children I once leapt off bridges with no hope of ever flying, but I say, "It is your responsibility to keep each other safe." What an unimaginable weight! I wish for more: for them, for me, for all of us to find comfort in suffering, satisfied with nothing, to nuzzle love without limitation, to want no more for more. Even me. Even now. Must we be so human all the god-damn time?

Dear lord, your precious babies are crying diamonds. Is it not enough to watch them sparkle? This is how we make things right: we pretend our pain is luminous, meaningful, holy. We pretend our cut, clarity, and carats don't stink. But they do. They stink to high heaven. One man's loupe reveals fiery flaws: he turns them over, inspecting until the cracks are innumerable; there is nothing left but jagged deceit. It breaks him open. Light blazes through. My angels, don't you see that our suffering is bearable and nothing more? Your existence is proof.

The beaches are filled with bodies. The boardwalk is filled with bodies. The bodies are not filled with antibodies and those are the bodies we worry about most. There are bodies in bags in freezer trucks outside mortuaries in New Jersey. There are bodies in front of cameras smiling wide enough to ignore 3000 more bodies every day, 3000 more bodies, 3000 more bodies, 3000 more bodies. There are bodies on television telling us to wear masks. There are bodies on television telling us don't wear masks. We need bodies to make money. The bodies say we need bodies to make money. Human bodies packed together process animal bodies to grow oversized American bodies, and they call this progress. Brown bodies are killed. Brown bodies are beaten by blue bodies. There are small brown bodies in cages across the West and a million brown bodies locked in cages sea to shining sea. Marching bodies fill the streets despite the plague screaming this is no way to live. There is the body politic. There is the body electric. Queer bodies, straight bodies, new bodies, disabled bodies, bodies sold, hungry bodies, bodies privileged, world-famous bodies, old bodies loved and forgotten; the graveyards are filled with bodies who could never be replaced. There is a body of knowledge, accessible to all, largely ignored.

And we were all famous. We performed sketches called "meetings" or "family reunions" or "it's so good to see you" and we laughed at the strangeness of the plot. There were wardrobe decisions, special lighting, camera angles, guest stars who made jokes about not wearing pants. It was very funny. The script worked every time. How we laughed. Oh, we got along famously — in front of the cameras at least. Behind the scenes things were not so good. There was general concern that the production would need to shut down. There was rumbling and consternation. There were meltdowns, widespread malaise, copious technical difficulties. Addiction issues. Violence. There were demands that could never be met. Cast members felt that management had left the building. They were out to lunch. We were stars, yes, but where was the director of this Warholian tragicomedy? In front of cameras, eyes scanning the monitor, we waited for the next line; waited for the plot to reveal itself. We twitched inside ourselves, anxious for someone to help or appear to care about us at all.

Oh sweet lord of molecular karma, inoculate us from ourselves. We have feasted on the fruit bats of your labors until we were too bloated to digest your teachings. We touch our foreheads to the hem of your skirt steak. We solemnly bathe your chicken feet. Our thirst is quenched by the milk of cloven hooved mothers whose blood we spill to feed babies whose toes we count with delight, *This little piggy went to market, this little piggy stayed home, this little piggy ate roast beef, this little piggy had none...* We beseech you, aid us in our boring hours of need. Most of us believe you exist — enough critical mass to tip the scales anyway? In any event, we're fucked, so please help. Oh great and powerful deity upon whom we grudgingly depend, send us a sign that we are your favorite fancy troglodytes and allow us to return to your restaurants and bank porticos. Rain down mists of antiviral nasal spray and magical elixirs so that we may resume our lives as they were. Honor our plea and we vow to ignore you less while we simmer here on earth, your precious little lambs bleating toward dumb slaughter.

Memory fills the vacuum of our days. I proclaim the word "surge" to mean "lonely" to mean "hopeless" to mean "frustrated" to mean "pitiful" to mean "alone." It means all the things we feel in the absence of absence: that which cannot come can never leave. I walk the hallways of my home issuing proclamations to the towels and pillows. They lay there in fluffy rebellion. Obstinate. I run them through with my broadsword — a fork with bent tine — which is only a fantasy because I will need those towels and pillows later. I am not that bold. I am a tinpot dictator of suburban angst. I stroll the hallways in flapping bathrobe imperiously dedicating whole wings of my home as museums of antiquity, mausoleums of prophecy, marmalades of marmadukes, what's the difference? When I run out of rooms, I name them again. Then again. I claim this room as my Chamber of Ghosts — please come, there is space for you. There is space for all of us. I am a petty tyrant, but oh I miss you so.

Welcome to the last day of America. Don't be shy, there are plenty of seats up front. It is duller than we expected, but there are party balloons and red hats, so shut up and enjoy. Believe in the white old days, we'll get back there: clear the decks, fill the prisons, pile silver trays with towers of greasy wrapped hamburgers and build walls higher than any 10,000 children could scale. Break the children. Break them. Break the mountains. Break the sky. It has been spoken that every creeping thing that creepeth is thine dominion, America, so fuck it up real good. The future is yours, more or less. Not necessarily yours per se, but did we mention the balloons? Once inside, the line forms on the left, until you reach the front, at which point it switches to the right, constantly. We regret to inform you that our capacity has been reached: you don't have to go home, but you can't stay here. Don't worry. Our capacity may be low, but our light shines brighter than ever, blah, blah. Here, have some tokens. If you don't mind a little friendly advice: never trust the hand that bites you; once retracted, it will do it again. I mean, it's not as if you didn't see it coming, America. The orange fox was in the hen house, but you only stared dumbly. You did nothing. Now bend over and kiss your purple-fruited asses goodbye.

II.
A Story About It

Superhero

A superhero sheds teardrops large enough to drown evildoers. But really, who is he to judge?

Sadly, after a promising early career, our hero hits a rough patch. The incredible callousness that citizens show each other every day hardens his tear ducts — tears will no longer flow. Adaptation is life, thinks the hero, as he shoves his cape to the back of the closet, then pulls on an old sweatshirt and gym shorts. But what's the point? After years of weeping, crime is still ubiquitous, malfeasance as inevitable as the Dorito dust staining the remote control.

Pondering this dismay, our hero points his remote at the evening news. Click. The channel changes and the hate crime that has plagued his conscience goes away. There is shock and awe. He spills his bowl of chips, tries again. This time it is a larcenous politician gesturing wildly from a podium: point, click, gone. Next a murderous cop who displayed all the warning signs, but was ignored: point, click, gone. A sex predator media mogul in a tearful bid for redemption: point, click, gone. All the men (and they are all men), one after another, gone, gone, gone.

It is miraculous.

Most importantly — it is effortless.

Our superhero drapes his cape over his lap and refills his chip bowl. He is back in the game. He vows, again, to rid the world of crime. He will train with the same focus a corpse gives to stillness: inaction will be action. He will ignore crime into nonexistence.

It is, he insists during the many interviews he grants, what the world demands.

Insofar as such things are possible, our hero is reborn. The public is positively ensorceled by this thrilling turn. They eat it up. On morning chat shows, they speculate that his incredibly potent ineffectuality must be supernatural in origin — it is the only explanation — willfully ignoring that his birth certificate clearly reads *Rhode Island*. No matter. The important point is that everyone is doing fine — wonderfully in fact — if you watch the right thing.

But alas, the world being the world it insists on being, tragedy strikes. The story goes that one morning our superhero spills milk on his beige couch while solving a kidnapping in Nebraska. One week later, the fair-haired farmgirl has been located (we assume), but it is too late for the milk.

It has turned. The smell is repulsive, disgusting. Our superhero knows that measures must be taken; sour milk cannot be left to spoil a room, nor spoiled milk left to sour a room. But what if, thinks our superhero, he simply carries the television into another room — perhaps even the bedroom? That way, he muses, he could solve crimes without getting out of bed. Performing heroics from beneath a fluffy quilt does have undeniable appeal, particularly on chilly mornings, and with some basic needlework his cape could be turned into decorative throw pillows. As far as the crime fighting thing, the bedroom would work just as well, he speculates, and the living room would probably take care of itself eventually, right?

I mean, it would have to. Things can't just smell forever.

Thus it is decided. Our superhero bends to lift the television, straining so hard a single teardrop forms in his right eye.

The Silent One

Only two nights ago I leapt out of bed to flail at bats descending from the ceiling. They dropped fast, banking away just above me. I could almost feel the wind each flap produced. That was bad, but nightmares aren't the problem. Not really. They started about three months ago: a recurring vision of a man stepping through our bedroom wall motioning to me with a long wooden staff. He wanted me to follow — drifted back into a cavern of fire, waving and disappearing until only his arm and staff remained. He sunk deeper. I crawled lower into bed. I did not follow. I could not imagine how. It was terrifying, but not threatening. Every night for several weeks this happened: him appearing and disappearing into our bedroom wall; face shrouded, torso draped in formless robes, hands and staff visible — the gesture — and then gone. At first I roused Anthony: my lips trembling, cold sweaty chest flattened up against his back. Anthony was warm, kind. He stroked my hair and listened, put me back to sleep. This was not a problem. It was a new problem, only days old, so it was not a real problem. It would resolve itself, Anthony told me, and I trusted him. In the daytime I trusted him. But each time I fell asleep the man appeared. Every night for two weeks, three weeks, four weeks... always late, very early in the morning, still dark and too late to wake Anthony. Anthony rises early and works hard all day; he needs his rest, so I learned tricks to control my breathing, not to shake, to press my lips together and squeeze my eyes until he disappeared. But he didn't. Week after week this went on and the better I got at stilling my fear, the nearer the man drew; first to the edge of our rug, then to the lamp, past the maple dresser, over the trunk to the foot of our bed — his body swaying. So this is it, I told myself each morning. I grow unafraid and he grows bolder. Soon he will be inside of my bed altogether; contact will be made. I was ready for this next phase, I told myself, but I was wrong. How could I be? Never knowing what the next phase would bring my preparations could never be sufficient. Still it arrived. The last night was the closest the silent man ever drew to me. I lay in wait, my breath hot and short. His fingers were upon me, passing through my middle, laying ice rivers through my belly, a chill over my abdomen into my veins. I knew that this would be our last encounter. I leaned forward into his cowl as a dark wind swept over me. It was nada, formless. I did not go with him. He did not come again. Despite the terror, I would gladly accept

Left to His Own Devices

It took Milton a solid week to get the lipstick just right. The edges can be hard to cover. He traced lips he had decided were quite full, pouty almost, with patience; left them glistening moist without blotting. In the background the message played loudly over stereo speakers: *Welcome to the voice messaging service. Please enter your passcode. Or if you are not at your own phone press the star key or press the pound key to leave a message in another mailbox.* Milton didn't bother to listen, the loop was always the same: *There are no messages in your mailbox.* His dress swooshed over the bedroom carpet to the first newly cleaned mirror. He heard her voice again, *Welcome to the voice...* staring intensely into his own eyes, he moved forward, backed away. The lip imprints remained; two textured pouches pressed on glass. *Please enter your passcode...* He spun away from that one to the full-length bathroom mirror, extending a leg for full effect. The lines were perfect as they must be: navy pumps, narrow ankle, low hemline, gloved hands, rouged cheeks, blue eyelids, bright red lips. He swooned at the sound, *or press the pound key to leave a message,* puckered tight, pressing hard against the surface. His heart fluttered. The hallway mirror was just large enough for Milton's face. He moved his lips as she repeated *the voice messaging service. Please enter your passcode. Or if you are not at your own phone...* never getting angry and never slowing down. There were three more mirrors left in the house, forty minutes left on the tape, yet somehow Milton knew this was a dance that never had to end.

How Simon Created God

God did not exist, so Simon decided to create him. Basing it on the earlier model, his first design was erected purely out of ideas. The A Model was an omniscient multi-tasker, however Simon's inability to comprehend the motives of its parallel processing skills stalled the project at the design phase. Dismayed but not deterred, A was scrapped. Work continued. On a liquid clear autumn day while Simon was raking leaves in his front yard — it hit him. Ideas, though suitably malleable, will never suffice. The new God must also be tangible. Spontaneous by nature, Simon began gathering leaves, twigs from the Ash tree, a molding base of thick mud: natural and tangible, that was the game. This prototype was successful but ultimately decayed too fast to gain the legion following necessary to launch it as a deity. Failure number two. The grant money dried up. Simon became depressed; indulged in a long repressed shoe fetish. He smoked White Owls and drank soda. Cried incessantly into yellow tissues. His wife, a good-hearted person, suggested a female-based model. Simon snorted. His nine-year-old daughter, a scrappy doll, suggested a video game. Simon moved out. He took a room at the Super 8, morosely carrying on his research. Strangely enough it was Autumn again that finally inspired Simon to create Model C. Not the land necessarily, but the colors. The green grass. Red berries. Black squirrels. Retreat of chlorophyll. Slate sky. The fiery genesis of it all right there before him.

Death in Unknown Throats

Don shot himself in the pews of the Monroe Community Hospital Chapel. It was a Sunday. The chapel was empty. I was out of bed well before I thought, *this night will not be normal.* It was 10:32. Janine was reading a magazine. I was reading, naked. This suicide, the news, was Joyce's scrotumtightening sea; ungodly information hit our shores each time the phone rang. *They talked all Saturday night,* from Janine's mom. Don and Janine's best friend, Sarah, were to be married on September 17. Now Sunday, August 21. Sarah had thought next year was resolved. It was settled. They'd move to Detroit. I stood just behind Janine, my large contours showing around her small frame in the bedroom mirror. Janine covered the mouthpiece — her friend Amy now — turned, mouthing, *Don made her french toast.* I pictured Don and Sarah eating french toast at 5:00 a.m.. I don't know if they were naked or clothed. Our bedroom mirror stops at the pubic line. For Janine, just at midriff. The drop kept pulling me back. It was all wrong. Don was going for a walk. Janine got off the phone with Amy and told me Don said he was going for a walk. He'd be back. But she knew, Janine said. It took a couple of hours, but eventually Sarah just knew. Called the police. I don't know what they said. Don was religious. Maybe they started at the churches. Where do you start? As the night wore on information flowed in dribbles and rushes: he wore dress shoes for the walk, no note, dressed deliberately, didn't kiss Sarah before leaving. But the gun remained a mystery. He had no gun. Sarah said. His roommate Jack said. No gun. But the nurses, staff, physicians, patients converging on the Monroe Community Hospital Chapel at 7:35 a.m. Sunday found a 9mm under his neck. Detectives dug the bullet from the Virgin Mary's thigh — identified it. It'd grazed the baby's round belly. I turned away from the mirror: Don was religious, this would not have made him happy. It was a long time since Don was happy though. We all said. Even me. He just wasn't happy, couldn't crawl out. I thought that as I listened to Janine take call after call, well past midnight, confirming, denying, weeping into my chest. He wasn't happy. Neither was Sarah. The shock waves of suicide spread farther than can be anticipated. Don was not my good friend. Sarah calls Janine her best friend. And Don and I knew each other in that way, through our wives. But I am struck by him now as I've never been before; the undeniable logic of this choice. A hospital chapel. Perfect. For a man like Don, religious, responsible, it

A Story About It

Three old friends and one new acquaintance were eating dinner at a local brewpub. *There was a flash of white and electrified silver wallpaper raining down like charged confetti.* Todd, the new acquaintance, actually said this. I'd never met anyone hit by lightning, so I was paying close attention. The current raced up the drainpipe and came blasting through the television program into the attic bedroom. It blew him off his bed. They discovered the wallpaper was metal based. A white flash knocked him onto the floor where rioting lab rats twitched madly through his limbs. He actually said *body like fish on land,* but I don't think that's as good. He's a computer consultant and maybe it is. Either way, his mother found him there and ran to the neighbors. Todd was only fourteen, the hallways were filled with silver confetti and their phone was dead. When paramedics arrived they located a small burn hole in Todd's back. At dinner he made them talk like surfers, *Cool, man, check it, it went right in there!* But by the time they reached the hospital, the mark was already gone. Todd pointed at his back where, he noted, it was like the magic bullet, same entry point. *That doesn't mean it didn't happen though,* I blurted out. But I always do that. It was inappropriate so I added something else. My wife listened patiently. My other friend, Todd's friend Scott, ate also and listened modestly. No, Todd didn't have any flashbacks. Not really, he said. Once while watching television with friends a storm came closer and closer until it was unbearable, so Todd rushed over to turn off the television and they all stared at him — it was weird and that was like a flashback, he said. I bit my burger, chewing. My wife was silent except eating and Scott was already finished. The waiter came and left more beer. I'd meant delirium, but why push my luck: dinner was good and we were talking and now I had this interesting story to take home too. My next thoughts would be more unassuming though. Such a delicate balance — one wrong word and all is lost. I would go for as long as I could or until dessert and then I would go no further. My wife knew this instinctively though. *There's actually a club for us,* Todd continued.

Fulfilled

Anton and I grew up in a small periwinkle house with the highest house number in America. It was official. In the record books. Men with hats and cameras would come periodically to take our photograph in front of it and ask us what it was like living there, having to address letters and so forth. My father was a prissy man with lacquered fingernails. My mother smiled too much. All was well. In the photographs we would hold each other, the numbers showing just over Anton's small shoulder; big, round heavy numbers that went on and on. Copies of the magazines and newspapers with our pictures in them would arrive from around the world. Anton took this to mean that he was an artist. He wore a cloak at thirteen — nobody stopped him. He poured Fresca onto bowls of cereal. He peed on the garden and sometimes in the sink. He was special. My parents allowed Anton these observances, but our neighborhood would not. Anton was mocked and beaten. His cloak was torn to strips; he was made to eat rocks. His long ears were pulled. Local boys did not appreciate the arts. Anton passed the rocks painfully and went on believing. He never did paint. Nor sculpt. Anton never composed a symphony or a pop song or an opera; never wrote, danced, or sang. He moved to New York City. Artists flocked to his side. Their publications followed his presence. Anton's plans and statements were never to be missed. His dream was to walk two lamas the length of the Appalachian trail. He would subsist on Skittles and orange juice for a year. Anton once organized a panel discussion called Artists kNeeling On Nukes, ANON. The press turned out and many artists. Anton was the panel: he took the stage announcing that he would detonate small nuclear devices inside of his hands and ankles, then commenced cracking various joints and knuckles into the microphone. After a few minutes Anton wrapped his dark Merlot cloak around himself and strode off to wild applause. He was an artist to the death: one autumn morning they found him splayed across an abandoned field outside a housing project in the Bronx, face down. He jumped to live!, the note said, not to die. They located his nails sparkling in the sun among the many bits of glass and metal, each one containing a single digit, but still not containing them all.

Hello, my name is Larry

I am a man of few bad habits, but those that I do have I practice with zeal. Acquaintances may describe me as stunningly damaged. I am a home. I mean I own a home. It is full of my possessions, tables and chairs and the like. I avoid other things. I have a picture window overlooking a yard that I own and all the grass on it. It is like my neighbors but we are different: both greenish brown to brownish green though. I am four sport coats with matching slacks and two nice suits. There are shoes that I own. Most contain leather and laces. I had a bicycle once, but now own none. A Mazda. I own a Mazda that is paid for. It takes regular gas and regular gas is what I give it. In my wallet are money, a button, two credit cards, a spare house key, a drivers license, and business cards that I am handed that are mine now. I make coffee, but seldom cake. I eat cake, but buy it in the store with other bread, meat, fish, dairy, fruit and pasta in the grocery aisles. I take them home to my cupboards until I am ready for eating. That is usually three times a day depending on the cake. Maybe four with cake. I am overweight. My wife is a shoe store manager who lives with my brother-in-law's best friend now and even though it didn't work out I am not angry with her. I am smiling inside. I see who I please now which is better than you may think. I imagine it will start soon. I will buy her flowers and a card, my new girlfriend, to show how deeply I care. Relationships are everything it will say and I will mean every word of it. I will clear some space in my closets and then ask her to place some clothing there depending on which season it is at the time. We will buy flowers together and plant them on Sunday after breakfast. Neighbors will walk by with appreciative smiles. Lare. She will brush my ankle and call me Lare. I will sigh and call her by her name but shortened also. Months will pass and when we are ready I will show her my ceramic duck collection and ask her to marry me. What a happy day that will be. She will take my name and we will live together in my house for many years to come. Our doormat will say Welcome All.

III.
Beware Deluxe

It happened again. You've been accused of insubordination. It's a recurring theme in your life and you will never outgrow it. There will never be a time when you are not driven to acts of insubordination. You have a history, as they say. There is a track record. You only have yourself to blame. Your attitude has kept you in a position of subservience and every so often you will be reminded of that by someone who really knows how to dress. You will both sense that you have a general disregard for authority. It will go without saying that you have a bad attitude. You will be in that position because you don't follow the rules. The laughable part (you will not be in on the joke) is that you may not even know how to go about learning the rules and then figuring out how to negotiate them toward some future goal. No one is interested in having you in a position of leadership anyway. A top-down management system based on insubordination would be doomed to failure for you and for whatever ill-fated venture you stumble into. The truth is that leadership would simply mean working that much harder to find people with whom to exercise your natural impulse toward insubordination. Which isn't to say there wouldn't always be someone above you. There would be. You would recognize them when they inevitably accuse you of insubordination. But with success those people are harder to find and once they invite you to play golf you may even feel bad telling them to go fuck themselves. It happens. Your best attempts at remaining insubordinate can be subverted by a well-made Arnold Palmer and casual conversation. That's why it's best for you not to speak to anyone who may someday place you in a position of authority. It will ultimately be more trouble for you than it's worth. It's also inconsiderate to dupe authority figures into trusting you unless you truly plan on making that next step toward middle-management and beyond. They are so innocent, these leaders working in defense of the natural order. They deserve better than duplicity. They deserve better than you.

Beware Deluxe: you crave the pretty lights, but the base model is always sufficient. I say avoid the undercoating. Enough is enough. A pisspoor consumer will always have too much. There once was a man who purchased so many fancy things that his coffin maker bought a yacht. There once was a politician whose Congressional campaign slogan — *Use Less Stuff* — earned him a job selling insurance. I say neither six of one, nor half-dozen of the other, but zero of all until one is enough. Bring me your old, your torn, the shit you don't wear anymore, and I will proclaim myself the happy genius of my household. I will dance in broken shoes. Twirl in last year's patterns. I will savor yesterday's glazed donut and laugh all the way to the muddy river bank.

This new path through our old forest leads to the Blood Pool of the Mosquitoes of North America. Thousands of mosquitoes perch their skeletal bodies around its rim. None drink; the mosquitoes of North America must constantly replenish the blood to account for what sinks into the earth, absorbed, recycled into flowers and weedy meadows: mingled blood of senators and orderlies, woodworkers, doormen, lawyers, flight attendants and waiters... The fat mosquitoes dip their proboscises into the thick pool and expel their blood payloads into its congealed meniscus. It takes so much blood to raise the level of the pool, these eerily straining insects. I release my leashes and the yellow dogs chase rustling shadows into the underbrush. I step to the edge of the blood pool, unfasten the buttons of my sleeve and methodically roll past my elbow. This time, I say out loud, I will give them everything. This time I will give it all.

William S. Burroughs came to me in a dream. Word virus. Interzone. It was not fiction. *El Hombre Invisible* materialized after reading his pages with a knife pressed to my side. It was not malicious, merely clinical. Dr. Benway made an incision with no emotion, no judgement, only focus on what needed to be excised. Perhaps it is true that William S. Burroughs came to disrupt a virus implanted by Control. That's what the routines were about you know. Those cut-ups and junk sicks. The talking assholes, clear jelly. Either way, I promise you it was excruciating. Pure, uncut horror. I screamed in bed beside my wife and fought to get away from Burroughs, while she calmed, "Wake up now, darling. It is only your sleep."

It seemed the man now worshipped a monkey. Monkey altars were placed everywhere around his home. Monkey paintings, monkey prints, monkey magnets on the refrigerator. There was an enormous monkey tattooed on his bicep and his sound system played only songs about the monkey. The man prayed to the monkey. He wrote books about the monkey. The monkey appeared in an adventure tale that formed the cornerstone of a whole religion. Millions of people studied the monkey's behavior and patterned their lives around the monkey's actions. The man's family were beside themselves with worry: *Monkey worship is madness,* they screamed, *and what is wrong with the holy ghost?*

Things to do with problems:

1) Throw money at them. Literally. Back up a dump truck full of gold bullion and unload it. Squash the problems flat. Or fill a sweatsock with pennies and smack the problems repeatedly until they stop being so problematic.

2) Medicate them. There are so many options available. Alcohol is readily available and socially acceptable, but there are far more pills than bottles of booze. Some people mix those together to make their problems go away forever, but then they are dead and that seems boring.

3) Screw them. Imagine your problems as sexual partners and have intercourse with them. This is guaranteed to multiply your problems, but the same can be said for all of these techniques and at least you'll be getting laid, right?

4) Meditate on them. This is a fancy way of saying trap yourself in a room with your problems and ruminate on them until you get hungry. Eventually you'll think more about food than the original problems, which, of course, will be another problem [see above], but easier to deal with. Just go make a sandwich.

5) Ignore them. More will be along shortly.

6) Deal with them. Address the issues head-on with clarity, composure, intelligence, and maturity. Find the best available solutions and develop the resolve necessary to stand behind your decisions and manage their ramifications with equanimity.

7) Feed them to the squirrels. Those little fuckers will eat anything.

IV.
The Nature of Precarious

A small house, balanced on a cliff, shivering in the wind, faultless in construction, surviving the indignities of our coldest hours: *this is the Nature of Precarious.*

***

A single tree, rooted in porous rock, stripped of leaves, witness to the vagaries of human industry, silent sentry of our days: *this is the Nature of Alone.*

***

A pile of boulders, more rubble than mountain, more barrier than bolster, the talus and scree of our faith, the skeleton bones of the mystery that surrounds us: *this is the Nature of Forgotten.*

"You feel so distant," said the liar's wife.

"I am right here," said the liar, "not distant at all."

"Emotionally," said the liar's wife, "distant."

"Oh," replied the liar, nodding to himself.

Once upon a time there was a very large man who walked into a very small house.

Or was it a very small man who walked into a very large house?

For certain, there was a man and a house. He was larger than many things inside the house, smaller than others, but he did not hold that against the things because they were only things after all.

This was a most reasonable man. He was not given to pointing out the shortcomings of such and thus.

What is the point, thought the reasonable man, of falling in love? This was a reasonable question for a reasonable man to ask. In a world where some things are large and others small, what difference can one man's love make?

There will always be things to make us feel feelings. The man was not immune to such things — feeling feelings — but what is the point, thought the thoughtful man, of such indulgence when there are driveways to be shoveled and the snow grows so deep?

There was a thoughtful man standing waist deep in snow. He could not for the life of him remember how he got there. But he shoveled. He shoveled nonetheless.

"I have needs too," said the woman to the hat. The hat did not respond. "I have needs too," she said to the cat. The cat raised, circled, and curled to sleep in the opposite direction. "Excuse me," she said to the water flowing from the showerhead, "I have needs too." The water made her wet. She stepped from the shower, wrapped a towel around her head, and rubbed a clear oval into the mirror steam. "I have needs too," she said to the reflection. "I want to tell you that I have needs too." The reflection studied her eyes — such a lovely shade of brown. "Did you hear me?" she said, staring into the brown eyes. "I have needs too."

"I understand," replied the eyes, smiling back. "Please tell me what you need. We are in this together."

"Love everyone," said the teacher, "always tell the truth."

"But I hate these people," yelled the student, pointing at his fellow students. "And I hate myself too."

"I thought I told you to love everyone," replied the teacher.

"But you told me to tell the truth," answered the student. "The truth is, I don't love everyone."

The teacher drew close, nose-to-nose, staring coolly at the student: "Love everyone," he said, pulling hard on the student's ear, "always tell the truth."

The old husband said to the old wife, "There is an accumulation of years beyond which I will not walk alone."

"You will live," she said.

"But there have already been too many years," he insisted, "we are down to minutes."

"You will live," she said.

"But our lives have become inseparable," he explained. "The echoes between each second are longer than each year of our youth. Can't you hear?"

"We had no youth," said the old woman. "You existed before me. You exist now. It is only one more day, old man."

"But what if there are no more days?" moaned the old man. "What if this is the last?"

"There will be more days," said the old woman.

"But how do you know?" asked the old man.

There was no reply.

"But how do you know?" asked the old man.

There was no reply.

"But how do you know?"

A toothless old man gave the gift of a tiny porcelain woman. Do not break this. If you drop her, she will shatter into more pieces than an infinite rebirth of lifetimes could ever repair. The tiny porcelain woman had been broken and patched, but the mended seams held together, reinforcing the woman with memories of past survival. The tiny porcelain woman would not stay on a low shelf. There was no safe place, so she moved through the world with her breaks unhidden.

***

The tiny porcelain woman arrived with a statement of provenance: *This is the dancing universe revealed.* The toothless old man laughed when he handed her over. I tried, but the woman would not live wrapped in a box in the attic labeled *Fragile.* I wept at my failure before it arrived. The porcelain woman and the toothless old man frolicked in those tears like children splashing in the ocean calling out through waves, *This is the tale of forms.*

***

A stone man held a porcelain woman in the soft summer dusk. They perched on a high rooftop closest to the moon with no dream of flight. The girl whispered into the stone man's ear, *This is the lesson of withstanding fear.* In one story, they crumble into dust when they hit the earth. In another, they float into space then explode as stars sparkling across the hot evening sky. In yet another they leap again and again into new lifetimes beyond imagining.

I am more interested in the dust on the photographs than the photographs themselves. Our white cake was in the freezer. I want to tell you that I threw it away with an old bag of shrimp. It was my fault, I am sorry, but I would throw it away again. The shrimp had turned. It was time. I find myself gazing into the baggy space between seconds: this is where I know you will not forgive me. That much is transparent. Your fingers clutch the purse strings for the ransom on my head. Outside our old home the treefort was torn down. Our last neighbor told me this. My confession to him: I never liked that damn thing anyway. It blocked the wind in the trees that swayed to whisper you were gone. I want to blow off these old photographs to reveal a new history, but history doesn't care. It is impossible. I accept that now. I leave the dust where it gathers.

Woo me with tedium, my love. Bathe me in the mundanity of your days. Allow me to savor the image of you scratching your nose, tapping your keyboard, sniffing an orange, transfering funds, ferrying socks from washer to dryer. Please don't tell me about your dreams; that unreliable shamble of the subconscious. I am tired of dreams. Instead, whisper to me of the seconds you spent debating whether to floss; unspool the saga of the waxen thread, the slow slide through enamel crevasse; this solemn quest to dislodge some rebirth of wonder.

The candle burns like this. Each drop of wax is a letter, each letter is a moment, each moment is a plea for tender mercy. The gray smoke whispers into your ear, *may your heart, my love, never be bound too tight.* The flames whisper into your throat, *each mystery inside of you will one day be revealed.* The wax whispers into your flesh, *what we long to hold quivers, naked, beyond the edge of suffering.*

V.
Epilogue

Do you want to talk about minutes? How about seconds? Hours? Years?

Meeting my kindergarten teacher on the first day of school.

Walking in darkness down a path lit by fireflies.

The birth of my daughter.

Her breath on my skin.

Don't you understand?

This is my life. It is much, much faster than all that.

Acknowledgements

Beloit Fiction Journal: "Death in Unknown Throats."

City Newspaper: "How Simon Created God," "Left to His Own Devices," "Hello, my name is Larry," "Fulfilled."

DMQ Review: "Once upon," "A toothless old man."

Lake Effect: An International Literary Journal: "I am more."

The Laurel Review: "And we were all," "Here is the man."

The Literary Review: "This new path," "One day I lay."

Pine Hills Review: "The disease."

Thanks to Stamped Books for publishing the chapbook *Discovering America* and FootHills Press for publishing the chapbook *While In the World* each of which contained pieces from this collection.

With love to Whitman, Max, Kane, and Little Max.

Notes

In "I pray you no more" the phrase "You cannot petition the lord with prayer," is a lyric from "The Soft Parade" written by Jim Morrison, performed by The Doors.

In "Dear lord, your precious" the words "crying diamonds" are taken from the poet Jillian Weise who wrote on Instagram, "Peter Conners is crying diamonds."

In "Those must be" the concluding line "You who go laughing from madness, to madness, to sweet impossible madness" is adapted from Li-Young Lee's poem "From Blossoms" which ends "from blossom to blossom to/ impossible blossom, to sweet impossible blossom." The poem appears in his collection, *Rose* (BOA Editions, 1986).

"Love everyone" is adapted from stories told by spiritual teacher Ram Dass about his guru Neem Karoli Baba. www.ramdass.org

In "Woo me" the phrase "a rebirth of wonder" is taken from the Lawrence Ferlinghetti poem "I Am Waiting" from his collection *A Coney Island of the Mind* (New Directions, 1958).

About the Author

Peter Conners is the author of ten books of poetry, nonfiction and fiction, including the prose poetry collections, *Of Whiskey and Winter*, and, *The Crows Were Laughing in Their Trees*. He has also documented music and countercultural communities in such books as *Growing Up Dead: The Hallucinated Confessions of a Teenage Deadhead; JAMerica: The History of the Jam Band and Festival Scene; Cornell '77: The Music, The Myth, and the Magnificence of the Grateful Dead's Concert at Barton Hall;* and, *White Hand Society: The Psychedelic Partnership of Timothy Leary & Allen Ginsberg.* He lives with his family in Rochester, New York where he works as Publisher and Executive Director of the award-winning independent publishing house BOA Editions.